Fix

Miles Salter is a writer, musician and story output since 2002 has included journalism children, running York Literature Festival fo *Arts Show* on Jorvik Radio. He fronts the ban _____ gang. He has also worked as visiting lecturer at Leeds Trinity University, as well as in schools and prisons.

His previous poetry collections include *The Border* (2011) and *Animals* (2013), both published by Valley Press. He also co-edited (with Oz Hardwick) *The Valley Press Anthology of Yorkshire Poetry* in 2017. His poems have appeared in numerous magazines and anthologies, and won prizes in competitions. *Fix* is his third collection of poetry.

Fix

Miles Salter

Laura
the book world's loss
is Westminster's gain!
Huge respect
Miles x
York
5.2.22

Winter & May
Books for Humans

York

First published in 2020 by Winter and May.

ISBN: 978-0-9931064-4-6

Catalogue Number: WM001

For Permission requests, please email Louisa Parillo -
louisa@theorangeway.co.uk

Contents

5

For Ruby and Fraser

'All writing springs from loss and makes its way towards completion...Writing gives us back the things that life takes away.'

Stav Sherez

Guide

After Max Ehrmann

Greetings, little one! Don't be alarmed. Plenty have turned
up before you, shrieking and grey, and just as naked. The
slippery journey from the tunnel may, at first, be a shock,
but soon you'll be stunned by what you find, and when
tiredness comes, there is sleep, the soft landscape where
names and tears are forgotten. On waking, marvels abound.
Milk. Things that rattle and glow. The delights of coloured,
moulded plastic: lift red hammers to your lips. You'll grow.
The light switch will be conquered. Letters will turn into
apples and cats. The dark months will be the most exciting,
a season of pumpkins, fireworks and outlandish fibs of
fat men in chimneys. Enjoy it all. Grow more. Shake hands.
Hug. Envelop everybody. Work has its place: make coffee
for others, and be patient with the photocopier. Listen to all:
even the loud have some wisdom. Sing in secret or public,
and so what if you're sharp, or can't remember the last verse.
The early decades bring a burst of energy and hope. Dance
fearlessly. Whatever suit you wear, you will lose allies
in unexpected ways. This is normal. The grief will stretch
you. You'll look others in the eye and know they, too, have
seen some precious thing perish. Be generous. And if you
make a mistake, as many do, remember the trees, the way they
are steady and rooted. As you age, the early joy seems stale.
Stars fade. Eventually, yours, too, will grow dim, and
disappointment may pester you. But know that you have been
a prisoner to nothing. Smile randomly, and do a little good. The
tunnel looms, eventually, a welcome friend. You'll begin where
you started, no sooner off than back again, a brief, brief song,
a fraction of a hymn. You'll struggle to remember this incantation,
until one day, little one, it will come to you in a flashy dream, and
while your companions are asleep, oblivious to your inspiration,
~~until one day, little one, it will arrive in a flashy dream, and while~~
~~your companions are asleep,~~ you'll get out of bed, startled, and
stand in the kitchen, trying to recall the formula. Close your eyes,
rest the tongue, and wait for this knowledge to return. Then go.
The sun grins at the window. The world is on fire. There is
so much you have not seen.

Date of Birth

It won't budge. Frankly, you might as
well get a tattoo with the numbers on
and label your one earlobe. And it's
weird, because you won't remember a
single thing that occurred that day.
You won't remember what your
mother was wearing, the drink she'd
consumed that morning, the clothes
that covered her and you, or the birds
that worked in the trees. You will not
recall the ward number, the doctor's
name, the midwife's emotional
response, or the colour of the
curtains as you flopped, wet and grey,
into schedules. Nothing will stay with
you; the groans of your parent, your
first yelp, or the debut sensation of
milk in the mouth. You will have no
clue. But those digits, the day, month
and year – they'll pester you, follow
you everywhere, drip from your nibs
for decades. Passports, driving
licences, job applications, parties –
they'll be a hook to hang yourself on,
while you learn about cars,
percentages, mortgages and grief.
One day you'll want that lack of
knowledge again, that pale, warm
indifference, its morphine mystery
and gift of selfish ignorance. And
when that news pecks your cheek,
you'll consider the moment of entry –
with its slide and slap and shriek –
and know, at last, that was where it all
did not begin.

Strontium Dog walks into my bedroom, July 1986

It's summer. A Wednesday, and four months since my
suspension. Mrs Thatcher is at large and my father
likes 'Lady in Red', God help us all. Outside, bees and
lawnmowers keep busy. Not much happens in Amersham.

I'm waiting for the future, daydreaming of girls and breasts.
If only. Any day now I'll see Queen at Wembley Stadium,
thousands of hands up for Radio Ga Ga and Freddie in a yellow
jacket, but right now, I'm lying on my bed, working through

a pile of colour that Andrew 'Texas' Yule has lent me,
hoping for a friend. Mega City One looms out of the pages;
Judge Dredd rides a monstrous bike and will not smile.
Rogue Trooper walks through mists. Halo Jones has

phenomenal hair and a robot dog. Strontium Dog
is avenging his friend's death but drops by. I'm about
to ride my bike to the common, when he shows up,
shoulder pads rubbing against the doorframe.

My mouth forms a black hole. The Dog mutters something
about puberty being a drag, shows me a gun. Three decades
later, I can't remember a word he said. The future's shot
past, its promises turning to grit. Freddie's dead.

The bike is history. The house where I dreamed was
torn down. I have no idea what happened to Texas.
The news chokes with paranoia. But look at Strontium
Dog! That stride. Those shoulder pads. How about those?

The Time Machine Arrives

Wrapped in cardboard. Amazon. Nine grand.
I've emptied accounts to get it, read mixed
reviews: 'Amazing to revisit 1985,' writes Jinxy.

'Bought Wham! on vinyl in HMV. Nobody
on mobiles. No Starbucks. George, Prince
and Bowie still alive. Gate crashing Live Aid

next weekend. Got a pound note in my change.
Nostalgia rocks! Drawback is bad headaches
but OMG total blast.' Others are more adventurous.

A historian visits the birth of Christ.
'Co-ordinates wrong. No star. No wise men.
No baby. Bethlehem stinks. Did we get the

wrong month? Not impressed.' A Vietnam
Vet returns to a remote village in '66,
makes sure his aim is wrong, undoes decades

of bad dreams. Women avoid aisles and bells.
Me? I've got a journey in mind. 1980.
Start over. Knowing what…that old cliché.

I'll avoid the slips. Make things good. I rip
into the cardboard. The machine is purple,
looks like bathroom scales. I set my destination

on the tiny screen, stand still, wait for vibration.
An antiseptic voice reminds me to remove metal,
remain motionless, counts down from 30.

Sickness rises. I feel scared, revisiting
what I've been. The room blurs,
and I'm nowhere to be seen.

Benidorm

There was a man with a guitar, playing to chairs. There was lager.
There were chips. There was pool, and time in pools. There was
a tooth lost in the pool. There were parrots. There was a lift

where bodies breathed Spanish. There was a woman holding
a nappy that a kid pissed into. There was a cross on a hill.
There was a library on the beach, behold the quiet readers.

There was a couple in a café, staring at football, wordless.
There was a man who looked finished. There were names
written on limbs. There were cigarettes bowing in sand.

There was sweat. There were the ghosts of Ted and Sylvia,
pre-Beatles, in a dustier, fish-littered place. There was Häagen-Dazs.
There was a sign in a window. 'Dwarf for hire, enquire inside.'

There was a speedboat. There were tears. There were chips.
There was lager, and blood from blasted, blasted toes. There
was, I swear, Agadoo, push pineapple, etc. There was you,

dear child, red-faced, as the hairdresser attacked your
matted hair. The way the audience clapped when you sang.
Not yet 11, and full of it, and wanting to go your own way

and become your own target, telling me to fuck off, but wanting
to be held, all the same, crossing the strange turf we stride
through, belonging somewhere, and becoming ourselves.

'Right sweetie,' I said, 'hop out.' I turned off the ignition,
and shuffled my child into a field. 'Little lesson for you.

Today, you'll be learning to forage. Could be a vital skill
in the future.' My daughter stared at the shivering grass.

No roller coasters. No screaming teenagers. No hot dogs
or Coke. 'Forage?' asked my daughter. 'What?'

'It's a life skill,' I said. 'Go on, off you go. I'll be back
in twenty four hours. You can build a shelter, too.'

A raven sat in a tree nearby. There were more protests,
but I believed it was time for tough love. I blew her

a kiss, waved at her face in the rear view mirror and rolled
towards Starbucks, where I enjoyed the free WIFI facilities

and a skinny caramel macchiato with extra milk. The house
was quiet, for once. I watched Netflix and chewed fudge,

slid the curtains to create a lightless space, and slept.
The next day I drove back. The field was empty. I waited.

My daughter emerged from the woodland, scratch marks
on her cheeks, lines under her eyes. 'I ate berries,' she

said. She looked tense. Perhaps I'd been too tough.
Behind her, dozens of children stepped from the trees,

a little bloodied. Some held sticks. They looked at the crow,
then sang a song I did not recognise, voices steep and shrill.

'Come on,' I said, fidgeting with my car key. 'Let's go
home.' 'No,' said my daughter. She shook her head;

her matted hair swayed. There were trees and birds
in her eyes. 'I'm staying here,' she said.

He was, naturally, in the woods.
I almost missed him, with those
camouflage trousers on. I had shorts.

'Are you Robin Hood?' I asked.
He stared for a spell, then nodded.
'Where's Merlin?' I said. 'And Little

Elton?' He laughed then, and offered
me some cider. The bottle was heavy.
It was sweet and I burped. 'Show me

your house,' I said. Behind him
was a sluggish tent, a dog called Rascal,
seven bottles and a sleeping bag.

We sat and did stories and Robin
released some cheese and onion and told
me about robbing a piggy bank. He smelt

funny and when I asked about Marion,
he went very quiet. He showed me a crossbow
and we aimed at quick squirrels.

Then Dad, breathing a lot, came
and took me home and talked loudly
with Mum. I had a bath and story

and thought all night about Robin and why
he didn't have a sword, or a terrific horse,
or a gang of laughing buddies,

or why he cried when I said about home.
Next morning it was cornflakes. I looked
out the window, but there was only next door.

The Busker

With buck teeth, banjo and a fuck-it attitude,
he had an uncommon touch, belting out 'Hard Travellin'' ,
banjo strings clattering against apathy,

spitting words like a folk-punk cowboy,
attitude snatched from The Clash and a tube
of special brew. A boozy scent clung to his neck.

Friday nights were best: chords ricocheting
off shuttered shops as packs of cheap lads
demanded 'Wonderwall', flinging single quids

at our feet. His dark flat was filled with ashtrays.
'There's been some bother,' he said. I looked
around his tuneless cave, and nodded.

Without Guitars, Sugar, You and Me Are Nothing

because their curves are etched on our brains,
and we have learnt the language of plectrums,

machine heads, whammy bars, fuzz boxes,
and because of all the things we'd miss –

The Smiths or 'Ace of Spades' or the ludicrous,
loud bit from 'Bohemian Rhapsody', or the memory of

getting hair in our teeth like we did at that Metallica
gig in '88, when I bought you the T-Shirt and said forever,

and you called it romantic before puking in the street,
and I was so happy to be away from home.

If there were no Stratocasters or Telecasters
or Les Pauls or the Flying V, our lives would

not shake, roll, rattle and hum. We would never
have moshed in the Camden Falcon

or sweated in the Town and Country Club
or rubbed together at high volume like we did

the other week when the kids were at your Mum's
and you said come on, we're not old yet,

and I watched your white hips as you slid
from the bed and pressed play on the worn out stereo.

The music came as we did it to 'Psycho Killer',
making a heap of noise, then laughed on our backs

at the ceiling before you said we should
turn it down or the neighbours would fret

and you went to brew coffee, blowing me a kiss
as you hummed down the stairs.

A Brief History of Immaturity in Popular Music

For Viv Lever

That voice! I mean, where does the moaning end
and the melody start? He can't stand losing you,
since you've been gone, how is he supposed to
live without you, don't you want him? As if his
balance and thread depended on the woman
sticking around. Those songs crawled from the
swamp of neediness, leading the blokes to stand
before a microphone and howl like deprived
chimps. Sort it out, lads. No more songs, please,
about crying. 'Crying'. 'Cry me a river'. 'Crying in
the rain'. 'The Tears of a Clown'. Okay, it hurts.
The manipulative sax solo has made that
abundantly clear. We know. We're all welling up,
honest. You don't need to go on. Why don't we
try some other approaches? Songs about
psychology. Religion. Clockwork. Medieval
architecture. Gerbils. Sewing. Cheese. There are
so few good songs about cheese. Or, perhaps, The
Battle of Agincourt. Put that into three verses and
a chorus. And while you're about it, can you do
something about the weather metaphors? 'Here
Comes The Rain Again.' 'I Can't Stand The Rain.'
'Why Does It Always Rain On Me?' Sure. It's
moist. Love is moist. It involves dampness. We
get it. But take a different approach. Write
something about love having blisters, about it
being dry. Like a plank. Love is like a plank. Go
on, please. Please try.

Fix One: See It. Say It. Sorted.

The woman's voice told us how capable we all
were. We knew about damage; how men with rucsacs
made ears and faces pop, or drove cars into legs.

Bins became rare. 'See It. Say It. Sorted,' said
the impassive voice. I wasn't keen on the vaguely
Orwellian vibe, the change of tense or the absence

of pronouns, but thought, what the hell, I'll give it a go.
'Rubbish on floor,' I muttered to myself, noticing a Snickers
wrapper somebody had discarded on Platform 10. As I stared,

the package whisked itself towards a pocket. My eyebrows
leapt. Doubting my stability, I went to the toilet, dropped
a tissue, whispered. It went. Satisfied, half a roll later,

that my new talent was secure, I pondered bigger issues.
At home, the traffic lights on the high street were bust;
I remedied them with a verb. A couple, screaming

blunt words at each other were, after I spoke, hand
in hand. A kid in a wheelchair leapt up, punching
the sky when I mentioned his face. Notifying

the authorities of my talent, I was scrutinised,
tested, then hoisted in a helicopter, flown to ruined
lives in hissing cars. I told metal to retreat

and brains to return to skulls. Fame came. Taken from
place to place to place to place, I solved every crisis and
fault my eyes could entertain, but grew weary of stopping

gunfire, famine, floods. I was jaded. Governments
gave me medals, accolades, cases of money. Holidays,
Lamborghinis and women were suggested, and, being human,

I was taken in, but grew sick of wearing white and holding
lambs that were (bloody) loud. I was besieged; incessant photo calls
and soppy choirs stood with candles near my gate. The Manager

of Arsenal wouldn't give up. After a manic four days
(seven disaster areas, three war zones and sixteen
dodgy WIFI patches, from the Hebrides to Milton Keynes)

I was done in. Healing the world was killing me.
Nothing surprised me or held me in its thrall.
At home, devoid of vision and breath, I forced

myself to look and speak. The cracked, imperfect
world returned. I wept, showered, exhaled when sirens
moaned streets away. I crept to bed for sleep, dreamt

of donkeys and Snickers wrappers, and, in the morning,
seeing rain crawling across the window, felt that old wonder
slowly return and, with it, my unexceptional life.

Perhaps, weighing the difference between gold leaf
and masonry paint, between worms and nails,
that would be enough for me to keep my big mouth shut.

Fix Two: A Summons to the Party

You're invited. All the heroes and punks
will be present – the dejected ones,
the sad artists, the fraying old women,

the prisoners, the dissolute, the bored,
the naïve losers, the boys with their blades
and hopes. Road sweepers, temperamental

chefs, alcoholics, toddlers, legal secretaries,
priests, badger lovers, Machiavellian mothers,
dubious academics, the buskers, the busted,

the bus drivers. The whole lot. They're coming,
most of them (there will be late apologies)
but many know it will be magnificent,

with crab and croissant offered
by clean shaven young waiters who
are available to dance. The invitation

states, in gold leaf, the time and place,
and the dress code: come as you are, or
as you hope to become. Tuxedos will drift

past tracksuits, tattered T-shirts, tiaras.
It makes no difference. At some point
inside the bash, the host will make

a little speech, declaring everybody
welcome, then go about touching fingers,
slapping backs and smiling for souvenir

paintings, starting with the kids from
South America. Then he'll point to the skull,
spinning like a disco ball above the heads

of the assembled multitude, and say,
'Look! None of it matters now! Corruption
is a thing of the faulty past. I've got a big place,

you can all stay. Let's have a massive,
almighty knees up!' And the party will rage on,
and you won't see pale girls with creeping

mascara. No arrests will be made. At a precise

moment, waiters will bring the liquid with its
dancing, daylight stars, held in cut glass tumblers.

Every thirsty person will drink and stagger
to their senses, and their haggard faces,
their pinched and stifled hearts, their loose

hands and faded aspirations will be drenched
in water and light. Do try to get there.
Seriously. You do not want to miss this.

I like to watch that show on television, you know the one, it shows brief clips of people falling over, or having accidents, or slipping near frogs, or losing their patch on the dance floor. There might be a boat, or a jetty of some sort, or a ladder, skateboard or trampoline. There is, almost always, a human, some movement, and the dry taste of gravity. The taped laughter guides me, and tells me when to giggle, and I watch the show as often as I can. Some episodes I have seen seventeen times. I know what is coming, but still I laugh and laugh until my face is tight and I am shaking and on the floor. When it is late, I sleep. I've been in this place for a long time. These walls are so lame. I want air and paint. But I have come to terms with my situation. It's safe here. There is no skateboard. No boat. No jetty. There is no possibility of risk, or adventure, or incident. I restrain myself from dancing. Nobody will be amused by me. The walls are my friends. One of them provides a window, and some nights I find the moon, and behold its face, and want to place it on a skateboard, or shove it, bewildered, onto the dance floor, or pull it from the dark air. I imagine an unseen crowd roaring with me, as I point upwards and laugh and laugh and stare.

Swamp

'If I crawl into the swamp will you wash me clean?' I asked,
but the person near me did not hear. They were on
the phone to the energy company, and anyway the words

were only in my head. For a moment, I closed my eyes
and saw a dragonfly, trees rising from a green surface.
I imagined sliding in with barely a sound, the undulating

reflection near my navel, breath halting within me. Instead,
I showered with something called Russian Leather and
went to bed. My wife read her book. Our breath was shallow.

In the morning I drove to work to submerge in another day
of meetings and emails and fidgeting with the window.
It was four days from payday. The insurance money would

desert the account, and so would the mortgage money,
and there was fossil fuel and food to think about,
not to mention holidays, water, requests for donations.

I turned off my phone and drove to a lake, remained
until it was time to retire and eventually removed my clothes,
then placed my wallet, phone and keys on top of my trousers,

and slipped in. Birds sang nearby. Shock. My mouth a cave.
Below the surface, it was hard to see and my ears
were full of dense, slow noise and something moved

near my leg and I felt alive and scared. I imagined
having gills or waiting in the dark to be reborn. Coming up
for air, it seemed wrong that I had not visited before.

It was cold. I could not see alligators. Trees leaned in.
There was nothing to buy or apologise for. A noise left me.
The surface rippled. My arms glistened with moisture and light.

Larry Jackson's Final Attempt

At night, neighbours glimpsed the blue flare
of a blowtorch, or heard the angle grinder's roar
as Larry toiled at his vision. The first attempt
came after Larry's Dad had been in the paper.
1956. The Grand Canyon. Newsworthy.

Larry jumped from the porch roof, smashed
his head. Through sedative, the boy glimpsed
his father's radiant white wings and swooping
voice. 'Come on son, join me, it's fun up here.'
Summers passed. Larry leapt from his high school

gymnasium roof with only a sheet of tarpaulin
for aerodynamic assistance. The ground was hard
and the ward uneventful. The third attempt,
at age 16, was beset by mixed motives designed
to impress a girl, who helpfully called 911.

Later efforts brought bandages, arrests and a long,
sagging sadness. Hair mostly gone, gut bigger
and spectacles thicker, Larry saw a man on TV
with wing-like appendages. 'A squirrel suit,' said
Larry. 'Goddamit! Hallelujah!' He got a second-hand

outfit from ebay (unreal blue, one owner, deceased)
and hired a plane. Above the tough dust of Arizona,
chilly air shocked Larry's face. Gasping at the altostratus
below, he toddled off the lip of the machine, opened
his wings and yelled, 'Dad! I'm ready! Wait up!'

Dog Lover

After Kate Atkinson

I found a puppy by the bins; dirty fur, tiny eyes, no lead
or name tag to say he belonged. An empty bottle lay
next to him. He whimpered when I picked him up. We
went home. I washed him, fed him, made a basket
from a box and a blanket, put it on the kitchen floor.
'Stay,' I said, sternly, and went to bed. He stayed, all
right. Those big eyes pleaded every day; food,
affection, a walk. He grew stronger, his little yelp
deepened. One bowl of chum was not enough. When
I read, he lay at my feet. At night he stayed downstairs,
but the whining became cruel. One Wednesday,
hearing a howl after the late stroll, I gave in. 'Come
on, then,' I said, and he bounded upstairs, jumped on
the bed, flapped his tongue across my nose. I giggled,
said no, down boy, but something inside me faltered.
He carried on. His tongue. I was transported. The
weight of him. The tail, thumping on the bed. In the
morning, we walked in woods, and I cut him free,
watched him sniff the places a bitch had been. Jealousy
pawed me. This has got to change, a friend said, over
prosecco and confession. She came with me, the next
night, when I pulled the car over inside an industrial
estate, and let him go. He drifted off to piss on a wall,
the rising steam ghostly in headlights, his eyes vast as
he watched us leave. Tears ran down my face. I slept
alone, went back in the pale morning, thought I saw
the shadow of his stain upon the wall, but he was gone.
I called his name, said I had a bone, then drove home
to a house that was huge.

The plane stuttered; we seemed lost. I bailed with the parachute, floated over a lagoon, felt sick with gravity. Fuselage smacked into trees; the smoke made my eyes leak. I won't say what happened, precisely, but I am aware of the sacrifices others made. I survived. The burials were as dignified as I could manage; the crosses made from plastic cutlery from the inflight meals. The wreck became my home. Birds sat on the smashed wing. I grew used to another life: the mud in my toes, the slow whiplash of passing snakes. I ate fruit and drank rain, went about naked. But after three months, I started to yearn for a mate. Please understand: I was young, and far from nightclubs and home. I heard him before I saw him; the thumps on his chest, the yodelling in the trees. I was attracted and afraid. Standing one night at the edge of the swamp, I stared at the moon that grinned down, entered the water, felt it touch my navel. Orange flames flickered nearby. I crossed, half swimming, through ripples and indifferent moonlight. He was lying on the ground, one arm around a chimp. I touched him. He drew back, startled, eyes ferocious in the night. I ran, lay down, heard monkeys shriek in the dark. The next night, I returned. The chimp was gone. The man was cleaned up, suited, sipping coffee from a white cup. He smiled, asked me to sit, but I hesitated. I wasn't sure I liked this version of him, his heavy watch, clean teeth and cologne. 'Where is the other one?' I said. 'The one who was scared?' 'He's not here right now,' said the man. 'It's just me.' 'When will he be back?' I asked. 'Soon enough,' came the reply. His eyes glittered. 'Hang around'.

was taken over a decade ago, by a superior
consultant, who pulled out the dodgy thing,
replacing it with a standard issue silicone
implant of (approximately) correct size
and circumference. I'd like to know,

come to think of it, where the original is,
taken before I went bald and lay in a ward,
twinned with a saline drip that pushed liquid
through a tube in my arm, until its plump bag
sagged and shriveled, like a see-through walnut.

Perhaps that piece is now on display in a jar,
inside a bright medical laboratory, where it is
frequently paraded before terrific young men
and women from Surrey or Berkshire, halfway
through their studies in medicine. I have no doubt

that, when they gawp at my floating, pickled
lump, they nod and say to each other: 'That
is such a fine testicle. Even with its malignant
teratoma, it has such personality. I do hope, one day,
to greet the man who once had it about his person.'

Hull as A Shakespearean Tragedy

The daggers are hidden on Gypsyville.
Somebody looms in the shadows behind
the betting shop, waiting to whisper

a word like 'knave'. The lovers meet
on Whitefriargate as Queen Victoria's
statue prepares a soliloquy above the bogs.

There's cross dressing on Princes Avenue,
a wedding is announced, then cancelled.
Bouncers loom at doorways, the ghost of

a tattoo on their knuckles. The final act
is at Hull Fair, where enemies with jewelled
tongues chew freshly poisoned mushy peas.

The lovers pass pristine Gypsy caravans.
At midnight, they leap from the Humber
Bridge, falling through metaphor and air.

Postcard from the Past

Hotel is appalling.
We are all in the attic.

My Sixth Life was the best

Serfs brought platters piled with nuts,
plump raisins, peaches. I gripped fruit,
and smeared them on my quiet lover.

Peacocks saluted me each morning, all eighteen
of them forming a perfect corridor of eyes,
their feet chained to the path. Nothing hurt me,

unlike the other lives where misery visited
inside seasons. That time I was a witch,
and they sent me to water. Or my life

as a soldier, squatting in a jungle for a demented
season, going home to needles in the park.
The second life was good but chilly; singing

with the monks before torches came and,
with a face of soot and tears, I looked to
heaven, asking if it was a curse to feel.

But that sixth life! The stupendous parties
and the wealthy, pretty things who came
to drink and slap my back. Nothing hurt

me a bit, and that wish my parents made
('may this child be without tears') had,
by some cold fortune, been granted.

My cheeks stayed dry, my fingers did not
shake. At the parties, I couldn't care if
the band drowned out my squads torching

the villages, leaving women and kids leaking
in doorways. That life. The things I achieved.
The trade, my ships with white sails. The way

I nailed the world to my will. The summer
nights where women laughed in moonlight,
and the peacocks cried out. Oh my.

The gold. The fanfares echoing
in vacant halls. That glittering life.
I'm telling you. It was something to behold.

Talking to Colin Ireland on 'A' Wing, 1996

It was quieter than the other wings,
with their noisy stacks of tattooed thieves,
addicts and - on the threes - paedophiles.

This place was for several, special thugs.
There was a coolness; they played snooker,
cooked meals, and nobody said how to move

in a crisis, or what to do when a man starts
screaming. We sat and talked, he and I,
and a strange feeling came across me,

of facing a soul marginalised from itself.
There was bulge and glare in those encircling
eyes. 'I killed two men in a week,' he said.

All of this was years ago, and Colin's dead, these days,
but the other night, on TV, a garish hour
elevated his crimes, and I thought of 'A' Wing,

the snooker table, what might have happened
inside those minutes, and, how, later, a man
was captivated. The programme relished the

tale. The cold, positioned cat. A monster,
they proclaimed, but I had seen the ordinary
file with a surname and number, read

about a busted youth, guessed at a separate
life; he might have thrown darts in the pub,
kissed his kids, introduced no grief. He might

have had another sentence, another pair of eyes,
and hands with an enlightened grip, busy in
a greenhouse, or at a flowerbed, helping life along.

I have nothing to say about what happened. It's been dealt with. I've issued my apologies. Things didn't turn out like I wanted: it was an accident, of course it was; the fish was being handled well. Esme gave me the money for the herring, she said to buy it for Bart. But, looking back, I should have been more fastidious, especially given the number of bags. More breathing, less speed. I must start meditating, perhaps that would induce better results? The shopping should have been less hurried. My mother was about to arrive. The house wasn't clean. The duvet needed attention. I said I found the whole thing distressing. The herring landed in the paint, whereupon the kitten got involved. I was distracted. My neighbour was complaining about the mewing. It's surprising how much noise a kitten can come up with. I know how upset Esme is. She's made that very clear. I saw the email. I hope it wasn't circulated. The kitten was a pedigree. Abyssinian. Spectacular ears. I should have put the lid on the paint. I'd been decorating that morning. Bit late for mother. Atomic tangerine. Perhaps the kitten found it alluring. Do cats respond to colour? They do watch television from time to time, I've been informed. Yes, he got paint on his whiskers. Thin rods with orange on. Clearly, if I'd been more careful, that would not have happened; you simply cannot let a pedigree cat near good quality paint. The herring fell in the pot, but I didn't realise this until later. Esme has been, up until now, a good boss. She was very kind when I was off work, after Mother's last visit, and even baked a cake, which was a little dry, but I appreciated the gesture. The kitten ate the herring, and the paint, then put paint marks on the floor, before choking, and vomiting, and one thing led to another. His body. The little pink mouth. Some sharp and tiny teeth. It was all most unfortunate. Esme was due to arrive three hours later. I know she's off work now. I contributed to the flowers. I've seen the emails. I've issued my apologies. I'm making enquiries about that sort of cat. There's somebody in Oxfordshire, apparently. The annual review is on Wednesday. Last year it went well. I haven't spoken to Mother lately. I am beside myself. I did get rid of the smell. Yes,

Bartholomew was a corker. The hall looks lovely. I'm so very sorry.

Well Hung

She found them in her cupboard; six, in all,
suspended on wire hangers, quite still, feet
beyond the floor. They smelt a bit, and blinked

at the light that fell across their stubble and nostrils.
How long had they been there, those dangling men?
She muttered, shook her head; then drove

to work, hummed to the radio's snappy complaint.
You Keep Me Hanging On. Twelve hours later,
water gushed into the bath. She nudged her toe

inside the tap, played with bubbles, washed hair,
poured wine, sipped at the news. The cupboard
was quiet until she sprayed air freshener;

a cloud of coughing commenced. 'That'll do,'
she sighed, then fell to pillows and a dream
where each of the men leant across her

with separate cheeks. She felt like Snow White
with a dwarf missing. A bluebird trilled.
She looked and laughed; the fellow

with eyebrows resembled her father. The baby-faced
one burped beside her ear. The third looked
like her last lover, the same sideways glance

and lazy shrug. One had a blank face. The others
were forgettable or wore tattoos. In the morning,
she inspected the cupboard. It smelt better, but there

had been a rumpus. Five of them were limp.
They held hands, clothes slashed, necks ragged and wet.
Only the blank-faced one breathed, wriggling slightly,

mouth parted in anticipation. 'Wait,' she said,
lit a stubborn candle, opened every window.
In the car, her hand paused at the radio.

Ashes

'Sooner or later the world must burn.' – Thomas Merton

The factories are dark. Nothing is made. Smoke leaks
and sneaks out of doorways. Dogs smoulder in the suburbs.

The Thames is a ruined snake. The Houses of Parliament
reek. The sky is black. Tyres burn. Mobile phones

melt in tickling flames. A library teeters. Paradise Lost catches
fire. This is what's coming. Count the days of retail and sunshine;

everything will be cremated. Lottery tickets, trousers, trains.
Cats, cars, guitars, molars, medals. Bottles, branches, brains.

Tickets. Teapots. Trumpets. Trees. Teachers. Taxis.
The whole damned shooting match will go up in flames.

The Flood

It starts with drops and spots, that turn,
within minutes, to a dreadful spectacular;

a deluge thrashing the land until waves
topple walls, turn paths to formless things.

It uproots trees, drags dogs and rats from alleys,
takes folk from their drenched dwellings,

their hands aching for the sliding horizon,
tongues thick with mud. They ask

for this not to be real, not now. It is not
convenient. Their throats reach out in waves.

The invitation arrived in a brown envelope, slightly
creased at one edge, my name neatly printed in Arial.
Elated, I rushed out to buy abundant gifts for the host;

chocolates, flowers, Star Wars Monopoly, a book
about Meerkats, an umbrella, a lute with all
the strings intact, a lump of Belgian cheese, a bottle

of something red and strong. I booked a tuba player
called Malcolm, and obtained some Jamaican skunk
from a man in Chapeltown, a large tray of pastries,

still dusty with sugar, and *Songs for Swinging Lovers*
on cassette from the charity shop, and carted the lot
to the party. I knocked on a door that seemed right,

and a man with a glass eye and a string vest looked
at me, wary. 'I'm here for the party,' I said.
There was nobody behind him. A television flickered.

The man shook his head, showed yellow teeth,
tore the invitation from my thumbs, ripped it open,
inspected it, grimaced, held it up. I stared

at the bill from the water company, and shook
my head. I turned around and sat,
despondent, in the car. 'Sometimes optimism

gets me nowhere,' I said to Malcolm, who puffed
at the tuba. 'I'm sending you an invoice,' he said.
'But if you want a party, come by after *Love Island*.

I've got some biscuits. Don't bother with the presents.'
I showed up. We sat in silence at his table for two whole
hours, only the tick of the clock making its way

through the dark. He was very calm, and I left feeling
like a small balloon rising into air, above the town,
and not too worried about being alone, or where

the breeze might place me, and it was only later,
when I was home, that I realised I'd not had any biscuits.
The aftertaste, was, nevertheless, impeccable.

Our new shoes arrived each February. We were
permitted ice cream once a month. Gas was supplied
in the better post codes. We were neither impatient
nor restless. The bulletins showed demonstrations
outside the supermarkets. Each fortnight, on a Sunday
Sunday, the drones delivered coffee to workers aged
20 or over. The removal of babies and octogenarians
happened gradually, and usually at night. The bee
count was broadcast daily. There was no need for
paper money. The rationing became stricter, but we
had to pull together. The machines had our best
interests at heart. The trucks took us to work. We
had everything we required. We tried not to make
predictions.

The Bomb Beneath the Bed

We climbed into bed, my wife
and I, pulled cotton and lay

in fresh dark. Breathing out,
I hoped she would reach for me,

but the door let in unwelcome light
and four historic people arrived,

joining us under the duvet. The bed
was crowded and hot. Her mother's

elbow pushed into my neck. My father
coughed like my wife. Somebody

muttered. Somebody snored. I heard
ticking, and drove a fist into the pillow.

Jekyll and Hyde Go for a Curry

Jekyll is waiting. Hyde turns up at the Poppadum
Palace forty minutes late, orders a lager, a whiskey,

and a vodka in one go. Jekyll nods, smiles at the waiter,
asks for Chicken Korma. Hyde wants vindaloo.

'How are things?' asks Jekyll. Hyde scratches
his stubble, looks around the room, one eye twitching

to the twang of sitars. 'I haven't been myself,'
says one of them. 'I know the feeling,' concurs the other.

'Out of sorts, ill at ease?' The drinks arrive.
Hyde tips the whole lot back. Booze runs

down his chin. He swallows, gulps, sweats, stares.
An hour later, Jekyll has a stain on his shirt,

the taste of vodka (or is it vindaloo?) inhabiting
his tongue. He quietly pays the bill, then leaves alone.

Fix Three: Fire

There was always fire. It was in your throat
and in your voice and fists and eyes, it
flickered in your words. It was bright

and it burned. Sometimes I detested it
and sometimes I longed for it, because life
was pale without fire. It touched everything.

The flowers in the garden smelt of ash.
The smoke came into the bedroom and
the kitchen; our food was black. The dates

in our calendar became smoking bullet holes.
Neighbours gossiped about the smoke that left
our abode, and at night we tumbled on the bed

among the flames and asked for more heat,
even though our eyes were streaming
and it was hard to breathe or be coherent.

'Hotter!' we cried. 'Let it burn!' The flames
creased our thighs, tickled our fingertips
and bellies, but still we yelled for more.

We wanted a furnace. We wanted to be consumed.
When it was done the place was charred.
I wept, but knew, soon enough, we'd be trembling

like pale junkies over matches, nursing yellow
and rouge tongues, trying to recreate that hellish,
insufficient roar, torching everything we could not face.

Said

I said I'm sorry
You said you bastard
I said I'm not a bastard
I said it wasn't just me
You said I never said it was
I said please don't do this
You said it's like having another child
I said we're better than this
You said the sex was crap
I said give us a chance
I said can you talk
You said I no longer want to
I said can you talk please talk to me
You said I feel trapped
I said I don't want you to feel like that
You said well I do
I said sorry
You said bastard
I said please talk to me
I said I don't want to do this to the kids
You said we already have
You said get out of my house
I said our house
You said you're selfish and weak
I said I'm sorry
It's just words, you said, you're good with those

We ambled out, a brief jaunt for the dog to empty himself, a pick-me-up before coffee, headed down to the river, kept walking, talked about simple things, the surroundings. A can nodded in the water, a boat went past. 'Let's keep going,' I said, and you seemed uncertain, but we did. Pastures, meadows, roadside paths. We went on, the land unfolding itself, and we ascended hills, perspiration inside our shirts. When the clouds and rain arrived I sat inside a cave, came outside to find you'd gone, your body moving down the hill and beyond my anxious, beseeching calls. I could see you weren't coming back, your back turned and saying nothing, so I walked on, into rain and valleys, feet sore, mouth hot, famished, weary. Seasons rolled past each other, autumn was soft and brown, winter was narrow and stubborn. Summer came again, and all the time I trained my eyes on the horizon, sad that you weren't there to share the journey, and knowing something had shifted forever. Strangers were kind, they took me in and gave me bread. I washed when I could. My beard grew wild and paler. The dog found an escape. Sometimes, at night, I glimpsed foxes, badgers, bats, rodents, all quick, willing themselves to go on. I wandered into nations I had not seen. Words spelt towns that felt wrong, I made friends and lost them, earned money and spent it, became a tramp, a beggar, rootless and sad, looking sometimes at my feet, the way they trudged forwards, kicking at the earth for years, bound by it, but finding each day the horizon expanding, and coming, each evening, to a town square with a half-hearted fountain, or a pub, or an alley, or woodland, a temporary space to stand in, and not wanting any more.

The House

Your shoes had walked. All the bits and stuff of you - vanished.
The space in the spare room where the bed used to happen,

now a rectangle on the carpet. The kids' clothes. Their books.
The house huge without you and the children's noise.

It's two years now. I've cooked, ironed, cut the grass,
fed the cats, sorted the gutter, changed the mortgage,

swept up, wept, made curry, slept. But still. It's all wrong.
Home is wrong. Come back, I want to cry. Please try.

But you do not. I stumble through the house, open doors
and close them. One day, I found a corridor leading to

dozens of other rooms, all white and resounding, and heard
you whisper. Some keys clicked in a lock. I wanted your hair

and voice, your red and green clothes back on their hangers.
Those rooms went on and on. There was nothing to be done.

The half-erect ears are gone, and the logo's
mutated, but seven letters remain, in blatant,
attention-seeking green, on her long sleeve

top, between blonde hair and buttocks.
For four seconds she walks in front of me,
and in half a breath I'm twelve years old,

uncovering old magazines from beneath
drab jumpers in a place he thinks they
won't be found. The glossy bunnies

recline in 1969, throwing back their arms
and locking eyes with the remorseless lens.
I can't stop staring at hair and lips,

tugging at myself, leaping to an ecstatic
space beyond fists and shouting. I'll be
besotted for years, letting things worsen,

until a ring is stripped and I walk into a room
where men discuss the steps. The woman
turns, offers a miniscule smile, slips

into a petite car, goes inside her day.
She's young. She has no clue. She turns
on the faces in the radio, and drives away.

Come on better angels, descend with voluminous wings and sort out this rough and rugged turf. There is much to do, don't just float about with cherubs and trumpets, we need a hand. Fix the potholes in the roads, the graffiti on walls, the clutch on the car, the glitch in the software, the undecided light bulbs. Fix the lines of dodgy poetry, the poorly written self-published memoirs. Fix the church ceiling, the boiler, the bug-eyed busted baby birds with sloppy wings, the lame dogs, the despotic managers with their contempt for coloured hair. Fix the rude and unwelcoming, the women who stammer, the men who swap their homes for the whizz and spark of slot machines, the fibbing priests, the junkies with their dot-to-dot thighs, the girls who dribble in wheelchairs. Fix the motorcyclists lying near machines, the drinkers with dancing hands, the risk-takers who slip from mountain tops, the billion beads of plastic in the oceans, the expanding universe with its appetite for dark. Fix the places where viruses are born, the women who ache to be mothers, the islands due to vanish. As for me, oh Lord, do whatever it takes. Saw me, stitch me, glue me, return me to 1971, start me again, take me to B & Q, insert a screwdriver, use glue if you must. I don't want to be like this, make me better, wholesome, a gleaming, satisfied, organised human. Fix fix fix fix fix fix me, come on, you can do it, only say the word and I shall be healed. Turn up with bandages, plasters, medicine, meditations, do your stuff, the blood and the wine, for fuck's sake, Jesus, I'm crying out, I'm trying, I've limped this far. I'm in the pew, my hands are open. I'm waiting. Come as a tumult of little birds, fluttering through the gap in the stained glass where Jesus has hands and a halo. The place where he touches a leper, that's where the missing pane is, and the gap's just big enough, miraculously, for you to squeeze through, assess the damage, grab a broom and make a start. Come on. Please. They're shutting the church in half an hour. It will get dark.

Therapy

'Stretch,' says Dzmitry. 'You're like a
prisoner of war. Swim. Go for sauna. Walk.'

We're talking through mists, shunting boulders,
pressing shoulders against the kids

we used to be. He's been there. Russia.
Totalitarians in families. He knows.

'You're like me,' he says. At the end,
we fix a date. I grow a little, and depart Zoom.

Shed

*'It is not true that men are unwilling to change. It is
true that many men are afraid to change.' – Bell Hooks*

His eyes were one-way streets and he could not
keep straight and I saw a man who liked to laugh

and it was coarse, sordid, quick as a fox.
I saw a man whose fists were too much to bear.

He wore good clothes but wasn't led well,
fed well, he felt peckish, hungry, famished,

was thinner, thinning. I saw a man who'd seen
hours of men on screens hitting other men

or killing other men, cowboys with holsters,
soldiers with grenades, men with orders

and missions to not weep or abandon themselves,
and here was a man who kicked at others,

because he felt little, a mouse who wanted medals,
who said, 'Where do you think you're going?'

or commented on clothes and hair and make-up.
I saw a man who was aching. I saw a man who

craved touch but walked through tunnels and could not
provide a name for the thunder in his eyes, a man

who had no sounds for the night or the stars.
I saw a man whose head was graffiti, who sent women

or children wet with fear because he drank and staggered
and banged their heads with his quick hands. I saw a man

who was a child at the hands of other men, a man
whose night plagued him but wanted to stay hidden and

untouched. He had lost his candle and spoon, but slowly started
to see through the dark, and went on a long hike without map

or rope. I saw a man who was waking up, and he saw me staring
and checked himself. I let him in, hugged him, and look, here he is,

shedding the dumb wrapping, letting it peel and drop, finally staggering to speak. He's naming his fear, and holding it, and look

again, look again, there's fresh skin, pale as the moon above him,
as he finds syllables and nouns and opens his palms to the sky.

A Trip To The Café

I was only here yesterday, for about three hours,
but feel recovered now, and have returned. I sit
at a table by myself, and order canapés, chips,

steak, scrambled egg, prawns, chocolate cake,
bacon sandwiches, pecan pie with bright custard.
I consume. I feel sad before the food and after

the food, but at least I have something to focus
on for a spell, and mayonnaise and vinegar
are soft against the tongue. 'All done?' asks

the waitress after my great bout of munching,
and I consider asking for more; apples, oranges,
grapes, olives, fish from the dark and salty sea,

chunks of cow and pig and sheep and chicken,
coffee from Columbia, cheese from France,
sausage from Germany. I wonder, momentarily,
about the taste and texture of horses' hooves.

The waitress is slim and has a good smile and I'll
have what she's happening. 'All done,' I say, and pay
the bill and walk through an alley with high walls

that go on for miles. I see nobody, and, weary,
lie down to sleep and dream of a busy house,
a woman who is kind and children who know where

their roof is, and all of us eating bolognaise and laughing
and the room warm and there's steam on the windows
and somebody asks for water and somebody asks for salt.

A Newspaper Lands in the Ocean

Its pages are like wings, momentarily.
Then, horizontal, it slowly ripens
with pacific moisture. Component
parts drift like landmass or ice;

domestic, foreign, business,
obituaries, the TV guide,
a transfer on the sports pages,
a photo of two mice scrapping.

A politician is gone.
An actor makes amends.
A drone kills a man.
Something is found.

All around, the rolling seas stretch far away,
almost lone and level. A fish nibbles
headlines. A whale glides in glittering dark.
A star blinks. Decades of stories go past.

In Llandudno, Kasmiri goats came down from the hills and visited the town. 'They are curious, goats are...' said Town Councillor Carol Marubbi. The curious goats stood on their hind legs in the evenings to partake of hedges. In Tel Aviv, jackals arrived at Hayarkon Park. A woman left dog food for them. 'Do not feed the jackals,' said a local vet. Rats pattered in New York City. In India, Swami Chakrapani Maharaj advocated the use of cow urine to purify the affected area. Cow dung was also mentioned. In Tennessee, Matt Colvin stockpiled 17,700 hand sanitisers and wipes and was investigated for price gouging, then helped volunteers load two thirds of his supply onto trucks. In Sydney, a woman in Woolworths got so excited about the attainment of toilet roll that a knife was pulled. In England, the Prime Minister was in Hospital, and two nurses stayed with him. Neither had any connection with the Bullingdon Club. Some adults worked on their last will and testament. People read. There was a lot of Zoom. Folks crossed the road to keep away from each other or had moments of revelation near leaves, sunlight and skin. Schools were closed. Couples drank at home, or said they were done, or kept away, or laughed, or talked more. James Bond was set back. The Olympics held their medals. Churches closed and the bread and wine became virtual, with some churches reporting an increase in interest. Easter eggs turned extravagantly cheap. Some prisoners were let out early. 'Phone masts were attacked. Lee Marshall sold cases of loo roll while parked in a layby, swapping paper for paper. On Thursdays, people clapped, or smacked saucepans. Wonky, colourful rainbows grinned in windows, upside down. The blossom grew again on the trees. It was white and bright and did not require petrol or plastic. The sun shone and dogs lay beneath it. Squirrels went about their business. The goats in Llandudno seemed quite content to stand and eat at the hedges while very few cars went by. They were seen as curious by some. The moon shone and people slept and woke and tides had small peaks and birds carried on their busy, hidden, musical lives, pulling worms and carrying twigs in the quiet morning air.

Comedy

For J.K.

We went for a walk during lockdown.
The dog took off near the trees and you said
'You do realise you could get fined? They

have drones, you know,' and we gave up
and I drove home and got salad from Asda
and you took a shower and then I did and we ate

carbonara in the garden and watched funny
programmes on iPlayer, your leg across mine.
When the shopping bustled in, I wrote a note

and put it on the Double Deckers. After an hour
of comedy, you suggested we go upstairs
and our tongues were wet and insistent

and I felt your body heave and breathe against mine
and afterwards held you
and the dog nudged the bedroom door

and lay on your side of the bed and the whole day
had been good. We'd not done much but both
of us seemed happy and when you played

chess on your 'phone I left you to it and later
you asked for lotion. I found moisturiser.
The note on the confectionary had vanished,

and you never said a word. Things changed
and changed again. Weeks later, we were on your
sofa. You'd made supper and we watched

Gogglebox and your hand was on my leg
and the dog stretched on the floor
and it was good to laugh and spread out

with a doubling of limbs, even if the pleasure
was temporary, like a glass of wine, or a stab
of laughter under a shifting Yorkshire sky.

Fix Five: Lockdown Buddy

*'Dutch official advice to single people: find a
sex buddy for lockdown.' – The Guardian, May 15th 2020*

Anna placed a clip on YouTube. Lying near
pillows, she pleaded, amused, for a gigolo.
No clothes. I called. Her daughter moaned.

Karen posted secret thoughts on Facebook.
Anybody fancy popping over for a shag?
I smiled. Chris went for a walk with a human.

I'm going to ask for a hug, he said. *I've not been
touched in weeks.* I nodded. My secret
buddy was due to turn up, any day now,

to slice mangoes, smoke cigarettes and kiss
me in a room with candles. She arrived, I think.
Before I caressed her fictional breasts,

I stood before her, uncertain. *Come on,*
one of us said. *Take that mask from your lips.
Touch me. Wash your hands of rules.*

Talking About Teresa of Avila at Poundland

24.6.20

It's late June, and heat spirals like numbers
in the news. Across the car park, Asda's
mob jostle with trolleys and masks.

Pubs plead for relaxed rules; beer sales
depend on men alive with humour and cash.
In quiet homes, people paw radios, then

wash their hands. My friend's sister
won't depart her house. By the biscuits,
a woman stands with red rims below

her lashes. For a moment, our eyes
lock. Her lip shimmers. I ache to offer
arms. 'Let nothing disturb you,' I want

to say, 'It's okay. Everything must…'
Before I can speak, she's dropped her basket.
Shortbread, soap and matches spin across

the floor, their possible owner gone. I stare
at what she's left, see each item resting
for books of years, until the retail park

is drenched in vines, squatting cars bitten
by rust. I glimpse redundant tills covered
by small hills of bird shit. I pay and walk.

A cashier wipes the spot where my trinkets
sat. The moment's dust. I drive home,
open my palms and try to purchase trust.

Where Snakes in the Grass Are Absolutely Free

9.5.20

Annabella hollered in the car;
'Go Wild in the Country'. I wasn't
looking for insanity, as such, but,

walking into trees and bluebells,
something came over me.
I almost cried when a bee

drifted past, absorbed in a life
without masks and sanitiser.
I sat on a sloping hill

and looked. Pylons held hands
on the way to Leeds. A car glittered
along a lane. A train punched

the air with noise. Sheep were calm
in a field. I thought things over, made
supplication, and wanted my life

to be noble, for the most part. I went
towards a new normal. An early owl
proclaimed evening in the trees.

Apple

A red globe shone in the basket of fruit;
its cheeks glowed. It seemed good.

Turning it in my hand, I winced
at the bruise that spoiled its darker face,

considered tossing the lot away,
then took a knife, and clipped out

the wound. Smelling the bright, pale part,
I nodded, closed my eyes, and got ready to bite.

Acknowledgments

The poems in this collection were written between 2013 and 2020.

Earlier versions of some of these poems appeared in: *Ink Sweat and Tears*, *No News Anthology*, *The Valley Press Anthology of Prose Poetry*, *The Valley Press Anthology of Yorkshire Poetry*, *Metamorphic: 21st century poets respond to Ovid*, *My Dear Watson: The Very Elements In Poetry*, *The Ver Prize Anthology 2015*, *The Ver Prize Anthology 2020*, *Poetry and Illness*.

The author wishes to express his sincere thanks to the following for their help in various ways: Rebecca Bilkau, Carole Bromley, Carol Ann Duffy, Antony Dunn, Oz Hardwick, Helen Ivory, Viv Lever, Jamie McGarry, Ian McMillan, Richard Morley, Helen Mort, Paul Munden, Louisa Parillo, Peter Sansom, Shane Strange and Stav Sherez.

Thanks to Jay Fleming for kind permission to use his photograph 'Holland Island House' as the cover image. The island was in Chesapeake Bay, Maryland, and inhabited for centuries but abandoned as it became submerged. The house in the photograph, built in 1888, was the last surviving building on the island, and collapsed into the water in October 2010.

Thanks to a trio of York residents for their help; Jim Poyner for the cover design, Seggy Segaran for interior layout, and Pauline Kirk for proofreading.

'Guide' is a re-working of 'Desiderata' by Max Ehrmann.

'Dog Lover' riffs on a story by Kate Atkinson called 'Cat Lover' which appears in her book of short stories *Not The End Of The World*.

'Hull as A Shakespearean Tragedy' came from a writing workshop led by Helen Mort at York Literature Festival in 2015, with reference to an idea by Ian McMillan. It was first published in *The Valley Press Anthology of Yorkshire Poetry*.

'Larry Jackson's Final Attempt' – the story is fictional. However, there was an air disaster that took place over the Grand Canyon on June 30th 1956, when two planes collided. 128 people died, and it was, at the time, the first commercial airline crash to result in more than 100 deaths.

'A Piece Of Me' was written at a writing workshop at the University of York, led by Peter Sansom, and was published in *Poetry and Illness* (University of York) in 2014. My thanks to Peter, and to Richard Morley.

'Benidorm' was written after visiting the town in 2018. Ted Hughes and Silvia Plath went there on their honeymoon in 1956. They both subsequently wrote about their time there.

'Strontium Dog Walks Into My Bedroom, 1986' first appeared in *My Dear Watson: The Very Elements in Poetry*.

'A Newspaper Lands in The Ocean' first appeared in Paul Munden and Shane Strange's anthology *No News*, published in 2020.

'A Brief History of Immaturity In Popular Music' - Billy Bragg's song 'St Swithin's Day' does, in fact, reference The Battle Of Agincourt.

'Postcard from the past' was borrowed from a Twitter page.

'Profuse' and 'Crisps With Robin Hood' first appeared on the *Ink, Sweat and Tears* website in 2019 and 2020 respectively.

'That Spring' was included in Manchester Metropolitan University's *Write Where We Are Now* project, launched in the wake of Covid-19 and lockdown, in the spring of 2020.